STEAM IN EAST SCOTLAND
1950s and 1960s

Images from the **W A C** **S**mith collection at
The Transport Treasury

Compiled by **Brian J Dickson**

Tuesday 2 September 1952. At the eastern end of Waverley station in Edinburgh, the 2.00pm 'Heart of Midlothian' to London King's Cross is in the charge of ex-LNER Class A3 4-6-2 No. 60096 *Papyrus*. Constructed at Doncaster Works during 1929 and numbered 2750 by the LNER, she would be named after the 1923 Derby race winner. Fitted with a double chimney in 1958 and trough style smoke deflectors in 1961, she spent time allocated to King's Cross, Doncaster, Grantham and Haymarket sheds and would end her days working out of St Margarets in Edinburgh, being withdrawn during 1963. (WSA82)

© Images and design: The Transport Treasury 2020. Text Brian J Dickson

ISBN 978-1-913251-14-7

First Published in 2020 by Transport Treasury Publishing Ltd. 16 Highworth Close, High Wycombe, HP13 7PJ

www.ttpublishing.co.uk

Printed in the UK by Henry Ling Limited, at the Dorset Press, Dorchester, DT1 1HD

Front cover: Saturday 21 July 1962. Looking east from the road overbridge next to Anstruther west signalbox, with Anstruther goods yard in the background, a crew member on ex-LNER Class B1 4-6-0 No. 61172 is about to exchange tablets with the signalman for the single line section to Pittenweem. Standing in the headshunt is another B1, this time No. 61140 which is attached to one of the four coal weighing tenders constructed during 1951. Both locomotives were the product of the Vulcan Foundry in 1947 with No. 61172 being withdrawn during 1965 and No. 61140 going a year later. (WS6246)

Title page: Monday 20 July 1959. In the background, the clock on the tower of the North British Hotel shows that it is a quarter to four in the afternoon, whilst in the foreground, ex-LNER Class A4 4-6-2 No. 60009 *Union of South Africa* waits to depart from Waverley station in Edinburgh at the head of the 4.00pm working to Perth. Entering the preservation scene, this locomotive would go on to re-enter main line service and haul many specials throughout the U.K. As was typical with the A4 class, note the type designation painted on the lower casing above the vacuum pipe and also the plate preventing the coupling from swinging too far rearward. (WS3583)

Below: Monday 5 October 1953. Waiting to depart from Alva station with the 3.48pm working to Alloa is ex-NBR Class C (LNER Class J36) 0-6-0 No. 65307. Entering service from Cowlairs Works during 1899 she would be rebuilt in the form seen here in 1921 and be withdrawn from service during 1963. Opened from a junction at Cambus in April 1863, the Alva Railway served the local industries, mostly woollen mills and a large distillery, and was closed to passenger traffic during November 1954, goods traffic continuing until 1965. The home shed will be seen written on the buffer beam, even though the '62C' shed code referred to the same location! Painted shed codes were a feature of many Scottish based locomotives. (WSA131)

Rear cover: Monday 13 June 1960. The second day of the joint RCTS/SLS Scottish Railtour saw the former Great North of Scotland Railway Class F (LNER Class D40) 4-4-0 No. 49 *Gordon Highlander* with its five coach train depart from Waterloo Goods in Aberdeen and visit the Macduff branch stopping at several stations for photographic opportunities. The branch had lost its passenger services in October 1951. Returning to Kintore the train then traversed the branch to Alford stopping at all four of the intermediate stations on the line which had lost its passenger services during January 1950. The special is seen here at the Kemnay stop. (WS4563)

Introduction

William Arthur Cameron Smith, known to friends and colleagues as Bill, was born in 1926 and lived in the greater Glasgow area for most of his life. He would be called up for National Service in 1945 serving with the Royal Scots Regiment and spend time in Triest during 1947 and 1948.

Bill started work with British Railways in the mid-1950's at the Glasgow Goods Rates Division in Union Street and later found himself based at Scottish Region Headquarters at Buchanan House working in the Chief Operating Manager's Train Planning Department where he was responsible for producing the Scottish Region Public Timetables. This kept him very busy with constant visits to the head office of the Caledonian Steam Packet Company in Gourock to co-ordinate the timetables and to McCorquodales the printer.

Bill was Secretary of the Scottish Branch of the Stephenson Locomotive Society during the late 1950's and early 1960's and with great enthusiasm organised many rail tours covering most of the rail routes in Scotland. Two of the largest and most heavily booked were those that took place in June 1960 and June 1962 organised jointly with the Railway Correspondence and Travel Society. The 1960 tour saw the use of the four preserved steam locomotives - ex-GNoSR No. 49 *Gordon Highlander,* ex-HR 4-6-0 No. 103, the ex-CR 'Single' No 123 and ex-NBR No. 256 *Glen*

Saturday 10 October 1953. Preparing to depart from Forfar station at the head of the 2.58pm working to Arbroath on the former Caley line via Guthrie, is ex-NBR Class L (LNER Class C16) 4-4-2 tank No. 67484. With Dundee painted on her front buffer beam and bearing a 62B shed code, she had been constructed by the NBL during 1915 and would be withdrawn in 1960. (WSA 160)

Douglas together with seven service locomotives. The tour commenced at Edinburgh Waverley on 12th June, took in Aberdeen, Macduff, Alford, Keith, Burghead, Inverness, Fortrose, Perth, Comrie, Forfar, Montrose, Inverbervie, Dundee, Newburgh, Dunfermline, Denny and ended at Glasgow Central six days later on 17th June.

The marathon ten day long 1962 tour took place between 14th and 23rd June and it ventured to nearly all parts of the Scottish system except for the West Highland line, Aberdeen and Buchan and the Borders Area. Commencing at Perth it took in nearly all the rest of the Scottish system from Wick and Thurso in the north, Kyle of Lochalsh in the west, Forfar in the east and Stranraer and Dumfries in the south ending at Carlisle. In addition to the four preserved Scottish locomotives a total of seventeen service locomotives were also utilised.

One of Bill's colleagues at British Railways would relate how Bill would be summoned from time to time to the office of James Ness, the General Manager of the Scottish Region who would impress on him that he wanted to see greater use being made of the four preserved locomotives that he had restored to running order. Bill was clearly only too happy to oblige.

With the end of steam traction in the UK his enthusiasm for photographing the subject waned but later he found foreign railways an attraction with visits to Poland, Germany, Turkey and South Africa to witness working steam in those countries.
Bill took early retirement from British Railways in 1982 and after joining the Scottish Steam Railtour Group was able to assist with organising many more rail tours using many of the preserved

locomotives available. All the profits from these tours were donated to railway preservation causes.

In the late 1990s Bill had asked the Transport Treasury to manage his massive collection of photographs which contains in addition to those taken in Scotland, England and Wales, examples of steam from Ireland and the Isle of Man. Bill's interests extended to the Scottish tram networks and contains photographs of those in Glasgow, Edinburgh, Aberdeen and Dundee. The collection also contains a large number of photographs of the many steamers that worked on the Clyde which were owned and operated by the Caledonian Steam Packet Company. Following Bill's death in 2009 the collection was bequeathed to the Transport Treasury.

The photographs chosen for this book, cover the East Scotland area in rough terms from Forres and Elgin in Moray to Aberdeen, Forfar, Perth, Dundee (all three stations) the 'East Neuk' of Fife, Edinburgh, the Borders and just over the River Tweed to Tweedmouth. It brings together some of the best of the photographers work portraying locomotives, normal service trains and some of the special tours he organised.

Brian J Dickson

Wendover 2020.

Acknowledgements

The author would wish to thank Robin Fell at the Transport Treasury for the opportunity to view a large amount of the work of W A C Smith and make a selection for this book. I travelled with Bill's photographs whilst working and selecting the scans and revisited not only places I visited as a youth behind steam, but also travelled on some of the specials he organised and photographed. I would also wish to thank Hamish Stevenson and Stuart Sellar for their memories of Bill which enabled the short introduction to be prepared. My thanks also go to the editor of the Caledonian Railway Association journal 'The True Line' for the opportunity to view the obituary for Bill which was published in that journal.

Opposite top: Monday 19 April 1954. Ex-NBR Class J (LNER Class D30) 4-4-0 No 62436 *Lord Glenvarloch* is standing in the bay platform at Thornton Junction awaiting departure at the head of the 5.46pm working to Dunfermline Upper via Lochgelly and Cowdenbeath. Designed by William Reid and introduced during 1912, this class were the superheated boiler versions of his earlier Class J (LNER Class D29) locomotives. Constructed at Cowlairs Works during 1915, she was named after the main character, Nigel Olifaunt, in the 1822 novel by Sir Walter Scott, 'The Fortunes of Nigel'. (WS2158)

Opposite bottom: Monday 19 April 1954. Ex-CR Class 439 (LMS Class 2P) 0-4-4 tank No 55209 has just arrived at Ladybank station with the 4.00pm working from Perth via Newburgh. With only two return services every day the rural community were poorly served by this line, it was therefore no surprise that the passenger service was withdrawn during September 1955. No 55209 had been constructed at St Rollox Works in 1911 and would give 50 years of service, being withdrawn during 1961. (WS3682)

Above: Saturday 12 June 1954. The 'Waverley Route' saw much goods traffic moving both north and south of the border and seen here passing St Boswells station at the head of an 'up' goods working is ex-LNER Class K3 2-6-0 No 61857. This Nigel Gresley design of Express Goods Locomotive saw the first examples delivered in 1920 for the Great Northern Railway and classified H4 by them with only ten examples initially constructed at Doncaster Works. Adopted as a standard design by the LNER, construction re-commenced at Darlington Works with the first of a further 183 examples entering service during 1924. Construction continued until 1937 with examples coming from Doncaster Works, Armstrong Whitworth Ltd, Robert Stephenson & Co and the NBL in Glasgow. The example seen here was constructed at Darlington Works in 1925 and would be withdrawn during 1962. In the background a J26 0-6-0 waits in the sidings. The very tall starting signal allowed drivers visibility of its indication above the footbridge on the approach. (WS3075)

Opposite: Saturday 12 June 1954. Having arrived at Tweedmouth station with the 3.28pm working from Berwick to St Boswells, ex-NER Class O (LNER Class G5) 0-4-4 tank No. 67268 is running round its train before working on to St Boswells. In the background the post of the stop signal is interesting, appearing to have a tapered concrete base on to which a lattice has been added. (WS165)

Above: Saturday 12 June 1954. A crew member is overseeing the filling of the water tanks on ex-NER Class O (LNER Class G5) 0-4-4 tank No. 67268 at Kelso station. Bearing a 52C Blaydon shed code, she is working the 3.28pm Berwick to St Boswells two coach local. Constructed at Darlington Works during 1896 she would give 59 years of service, being withdrawn in 1955. 'The Tweed Valley' line had been opened to serve the rich agricultural countryside between St Boswells and Tweedmouth in two sections. In July 1849 the York, Newcastle and Berwick Railway opened the section between Tweedmouth and Sprouston with the North British Railway opening the section from St Boswells to Kelso and making a head on connection at Sprouston in June 1851. By the time of these photographs the service consisted of two return trips per day between St Boswells and Berwick with three return services per day between St Boswells and Kelso. Five stations on the line had their passenger services withdrawn in July 1955 and in June 1964 all passenger services were withdrawn. Goods traffic continued until withdrawn in March 1965 between Tweedmouth and Kelso and March 1968 between Kelso and St Boswells. These were the days when a railwayman might also walk on the line without the requirement for high visibility clothing. (WS2651)

Opposite top: Saturday 12 June 1954. Another ex-LNER Class K3 2-6-0 is here seen at Tweedmouth shed. No. 61969 entered service from Darlington Works during 1936 and would be withdrawn only 26 years later in 1962. (WS2248)

Opposite bottom: Saturday 21 May 1955. Ex-LNER Class D49/1 4-4-0 No. 62718 *Kinross-shire* is seen departing from St Boswells station with the 4.10pm local from Edinburgh Waverley to Hawick. Entering service from Darlington Works during 1928 she would spend her working life based at Scottish sheds, being finally allocated to St Margarets in Edinburgh and withdrawn in 1961. The Nigel Gresley designed three cylinder Class D49 locomotives appeared from Darlington Works between 1927 and 1935 with a total of 76 examples being constructed. The class became commonly known as 'Shires' or 'Hunts' depending on the name applied and were constructed utilising three differing types of valve gear. Part 1 locomotives used conventional piston valves whilst part 2 were fitted with Lentz rotary cam operated poppet valves and part 3 locomotives with Lentz oscillating cam operated poppet valves. (WS3488)

Above: Saturday 12 June 1954. Also seen in Tweedmouth shed yard is ex-NBR Class J (LNER Class D30) 'Superheated Scott' 4-4-0 No. 62424 *Claverhouse*. Constructed at Cowlairs Works during 1914, she would be withdrawn from service in 1957. The 7th Laird of Claverhouse, also known as 'Bonnie Dundee', is the subject of the poem written by Sir Walter Scott in 1825. He is also mentioned in the Scott novel 'Old Mortality' published in 1816. No. 62424 shows much evidence of hard work judging from the lack of paint burnt away on the lower portion of the smokebox. This would be caused by an accumulation of ash and cinders within but at such a high level would probably impair steaming as it would cover the ends of the lower tubes. The same grey ash stains this time from smokebox emptying are apparent on the front framing as well. (WS2247)

Opposite top: Saturday 28 August 1954. Standing adjacent to the turntable at the former North British Railway shed at Stirling, Shore Road is ex-NBR Class B (LNER Class J37) 0-6-0 No. 64585. Bearing the correct 63B shed code, she had been constructed by the NBL during 1918 and would be withdrawn in 1964 having given 46 years of service. The former NBR shed at Shore Road closed during September 1957 with its allocation of locomotives moving across town to the former CR Burghmuir or Stirling South shed, located just south of Stirling station. Lying within the LMS Northern Division, Stirling South was initially allocated the code of 31B but became 29B in 1935. British Railways continued the former LMS code system but allocated 63B again changed to 65J in 1960, Closed to steam power in June 1960, Stirling South was later demolished. (WS111)

Opposite bottom: Saturday 28 August 1954. Sandwiched within a row of locomotives at Thornton Junction shed and still bearing its former owners identity is ex-NBR Class M (LNER Class C15) 4-4-2 tank No. 7461. Constructed by the Yorkshire Engine Co during 1912 and numbered 141 by the NBR, she would become No. 9141 and later 7461 with the LNER. Destined never to gain its British Railways identity she would be withdrawn from service on 31 July 1954. In 1954 Thornton Junction was a fairly modern affair at just over 20 years old, it also had a 70 foot turntable. It BR days it was 62A and it was to here that a large number of former NBR and LNER 0-6-0 types were based on duties mainly involving the huge amounts of coal coming from the surrounding collieries. The shed lasted until April 1967 and was later demolished. (WS202)

Above: Saturday 28 August 1954. Seen here a long way from its original home territory, ex-GER Class R24 (LNER Class J69) 0-6-0 tank No. 68504 is parked in the yard at Thornton Junction shed. Originally constructed at Stratford Works in 1890, she would be rebuilt during 1902 and transferred to the Scottish Area of the LNER in the late 1920s and utilised on shunting duties. She would be withdrawn from service during 1956. The crane in the background is not indentified. (WS156)

Saturday 28 August 1954. Seen departing from Dundee West station with the 11.35am working to Glasgow via Perth containing through coaches to London, are ex-LMS Class 5 4-6-0 No. 44786 leading classmate No. 44677. Both locomotives were constructed at Horwich Works, the former during 1947 and the latter post-nationalisation in 1950. No. 44677 was paired with a coal-weighing tender so that usage might be measured. It was also fitted with roller bearings on the centre driving axle and intended to give better service. Neither locomotive had long working lives with No. 44786 being withdrawn in 1966 and No. 44677 during 1967. The Dundee and Perth Railway was opened in May 1847 and served a station situated close to the later named Dundee West station. The D&PR was absorbed by the Scottish Central Railway in 1863 with the SCR itself being absorbed into the Caledonian Railway in 1865, It would be 1880 before the new Dundee West station was opened to traffic with the frontage and office constructed in the grand Scottish Baronial style using red sandstone. The 1951 BR Scottish Region timetable shows a healthy 14 return services to Perth each weekday together with connecting services to London Euston. Despite this the station closed to all traffic in May 1965 and was demolished the following year. (WS2192)

Saturday 28 August 1954. Designed by William Reid and introduced during 1913, his 'Superheated Intermediate' Class K 4-4-0s for the NBR were all named after Glens situated throughout the NBR territory and subsequently simply became known as the 'Glen' class. Classified D34 by the LNER a total of 32 examples were constructed all at Cowlairs Works between 1913 and 1920. Originally numbered 407 by the NBR she would become No. 9407 and later 2475 with the LNER. Waiting to depart from Thornton Junction at the head of the 12.46pm Dundee Tay Bridge to Edinburgh Waverley 'stopper' is No. 62475 *Glen Beasdale.* Entering service in 1913 she would be withdrawn during 1959. (WS2303)

Opposite top: Saturday 4 September 1954. Standing in a headshunt at Perth shed in a rather forlorn state is ex-LMS Class 4P 4-4-0 'Compound' No. 40923. Constructed by the Vulcan Foundry during 1927 she was destined to be withdrawn during the month following this photograph, October 1954. (WS637)

Opposite bottom: Saturday 4 September 1954. The John McIntosh designed 'Dunalastair' series of 4-4-0 express passenger locomotives for the Caledonian Railway proved themselves to be reliant and efficient classes handling all the 'Anglo-Scottish' passenger traffic for many years before the introduction of larger locomotives. Relegated to minor duties with British Railways, 'Dunalastair IV' Class No. 54448 is seen here at Stirling station waiting to depart with the 2.45pm service to Alloa. Entering service from St Rollox Works in 1912 she would be withdrawn during 1955. (WS696)

Above: Tuesday 7 September 1954. Departing from the cavernous gloom of Princes Street station in Edinburgh at the head of the 4.05pm working to Carstairs with through coaches to Liverpool Exchange, is ex-LMS Class 4P 2-6-4 tank No. 42270. Entering service from Derby Works in 1947 she would be allocated new to Dalry Road shed in Edinburgh. Ending her days based at Chester shed she would be withdrawn during 1963. These Charles Fairburn designed locomotives were a derivative of the earlier William Stanier design incorporating a shorter wheelbase. A total of 277 examples were constructed coming from both Derby and Brighton Works between 1945 and 1951. Two found their way into the preservation scene, both based at the Lakeside and Haverthwaite Railway. This grand station constructed between 1890 and 1893 replaced earlier inferior structures that had been opened by the Caledonian Railway in 1848 and 1870. With an enormous roof spanning seven platforms the station was fronted in 1903 with the opening of the 'Caledonian Hotel' which worked in direct competition with the 'North British Hotel' at the opposite end of Princes Street which adjoined Waverley station run by the North British Railway. (WS573)

Opposite: Saturday 11 September 1954. Waiting to depart from Fraserburgh station with the 3.00pm working to Aberdeen is BR Standard Class 4 2-6-4 tank No. 80005. Constructed at Derby Works during 1952 and allocated new to Kittybrewster shed in Aberdeen, she would end her days based at Polmadie shed in Glasgow and be withdrawn after only 14 years of service in 1966. Fraserburgh was reached by the Formartine and Buchan Railway in April 1865 with passenger services being withdrawn one hundred years later in 1965. Goods traffic continued until withdrawal in 1979. The tower in the background belongs to the Dalrymple Hall which was constructed during 1881. It was sold to Fraserburgh town council in 1945 and is still a prominent building in the town. (WS2762)

Above: Saturday 11 September 1954. Waiting to depart from Aberdeen station at the head of the 5.30pm 'Granite City' to Glasgow Buchanan Street is BR Standard Class 5 4-6-0 No. 73007. Entering service from Derby Works in 1951 she was allocated new to Perth shed and is carrying the correct 63A shed code. Being re-allocated to Stirling in the mid-1960 she would be withdrawn from service during 1966. With their basic design based on the former LMS Class 5 4-6-0s, the 'Black Fives', the British Railways Standard 5MT locomotives incorporated a number of applications to assist their crews with preparation and disposal. A total of one hundred and 172 examples were constructed between 1951 and 1957 with 130 coming out of Derby Works and 42 entering service from Doncaster Works. Of the Derby examples 30 were fitted with British Caprotti valve gear. (WS2173)

Above: Saturday 11 September 1954. Class B1 4-6-0 No. 61352 is waiting to depart from Elgin station with the 9.25am working to Aberdeen via the coast line which re-joined the main direct line at Cairnie Junction. Entering service post-nationalisation in 1949 from Darlington Works she was allocated new to Kittybrewster shed in Aberdeen, but would only give 13 years service before being withdrawn in 1962. (WS2764)

Opposite top: Saturday 18 December 1954. With a full head of steam ex-NBR Class L (LNER Class C16) 4-4-2 tank No. 67490 is ready to depart from Perth station at the head of the 12.05pm local to Dundee West. Designed by William Reid as the superheated boiler version of his earlier Class M (LNER Class C15) locomotives, a total of 21 were delivered by the NBL between 1915 and 1921. No. 67490 was from a 1916 batch that would be withdrawn from service during 1960. (WS206)

Bottom: Saturday 18 December 1954. At Dundee East station ex-NBR Class J 'Superheated Scott' (LNER Class D30) 4-4-0 No. 62434 *Kettledrummie* is preparing to depart with the 1.08pm local to Forfar using the former Caledonian Railway direct line via Monikie and Kirkbuddo. This route was due to close to passenger traffic three weeks later on Saturday 8 January 1955. Constructed at Cowlairs Works in 1915 and named after a preacher in the Sir Walter Scott work 'Old Mortality', No. 62434 would end her days based at Dundee Tay Bridge shed and be withdrawn in 1958. (WS2189)

Above: Saturday 8 January 1955. This last day of the passenger service from Dundee West station to Blairgowrie via Lochee, Newtyle and Coupar Angus sees ex-LNER Class B1 4-6-0 No. 61101 preparing to depart with the 1.12pm working. Perhaps it is the Guard we can see consulting his watch prior to departure. Constructed by the NBL during 1946 she would be allocated new to Dundee Tay Bridge shed but would end her days working out of Dunfermline Upper shed until withdrawn in 1966. (WS20)

Opposite top: Saturday 8 January 1955. Waiting to depart from Dundee East station with the 12.19pm stopper to Barnhill is ex-NBR Class L (LNER Class C16) 4-4-2 tank No. 67493. Entering service from the NBL during 1916 she would be withdrawn in 1956. This was the last day of passenger services on this ex-Caledonian Railway route to Forfar from its junction at Broughty Ferry. (WS2636)

Opposite bottom: Having reached Barnhill, No 67493 has run round its two coaches and is preparing to return to Dundee East as the 12.41pm departure. Note that the signalman is handing the single line tablet to a crew member. The Dundee and Forfar Direct Railway was owned by the Caley and its route from Dundee East to Forfar, from a junction at Broughty Ferry was opened during November 1870 with three intermediate stations; Kilgennie, Kirkbuddo, and Kingsmuir. Barnhill station on the outskirts of Dundee was not opened until October 1874. Following the end of passengers services in January 1955, goods services continued until November 1967 after which came complete closure and demolition. (WS2637)

Above: Saturday 8 January 1955. Ex-NBR Class G (LNER Class Y9) 0-4-0 saddle tank No. 68108 is seen working within the Dundee Harbour Trust lines near Camperdown Junction, Dundee. The primitive but reasonably successful spark arrester will be noted. Constructed at Cowlairs Works during 1890 and later paired with a wooden coal tender as seen here, she would give 69 years of service being withdrawn in 1959. (WS3726)

Opposite top: Saturday 22 January 1955. Bearing a 64A St Margarets shed code, ex-NBR Class L (LNER Class C16) 4-4-2 tank No. 67495 is waiting to work the 3.10pm departure to Polmont from the single platform at Grangemouth station. Constructed by the NBL during 1916 she would be withdrawn 40 years later in 1956. This William Reid design was a superheated version of his earlier Class M (LNER Class C15) locomotives. (WS2386)

Opposite bottom: Saturday 26 February 1955. With a recent snowfall still on the ground, ex-NBR Class M (LNER Class C15) 4-4-2 tank No. 67459 is standing in the west bay platform at Polmont station and is preparing to depart with the 10.52am working to Falkirk Grahamston which includes a parcels van at the head. Constructed by the Yorkshire Engine Co during 1912 she would be withdrawn from service eight months after this photograph in October 1955. (WS213

Above: Saturday 26 February 1955. This wintry scene shows No. 67495 again, this time waiting to depart from Bo'ness station at the head of the 1.57pm working to Polmont. Services to this station were sparse with only four return trains each weekday and it would be during May 1956 when the passenger services were withdrawn. (WS3587)

Opposite top: Saturday 26 February 1955. Polmont shed lay to the west of the station and below the level of the Union Canal from whose towpath this photograph has been taken. The panoramic view shows the shed on the left with Class J36 No. 65290 standing next to the coaling stage in front of Class 4MT 'Mogul' No. 43140. In the background, Class D11 No. 62689. *Maid of Lorn* is hauling the 10.55am Thornton Junction to Glasgow Queen Street passenger train and Class J35 No. 64258 is heading an eastbound goods train. (WS42)

Bottom: Saturday 26 February 1955. This splendid photograph shows ex-LNER Class A3
4-6-2 No. 60101 *Cicero* working hard at the head of the eleven coach 11.00am working from Glasgow
Queen Street to Edinburgh Waverley as it leaves Polmont station in the background. Constructed at
Doncaster Works during 1930 and numbered 2797 by the LNER, she was allocated new to Haymarket shed
in Edinburgh and was based there for the bulk of her working life until withdrawn in 1963 whilst based at
St Margarets shed in Edinburgh. (WS56)

Opposite: Saturday 12 March 1955. At the head of the 4.10pm local from Dundee West to Perth, ex-LNER Class D49 4-4-0 No. 62706 *Forfarshire* has steam to spare as it crosses the River Tay on the approach to Perth station with its three coach train. This single track bridge on the former Dundee and Perth Railway was constructed during 1864 and replaced an earlier timber structure. The D&PR had reached the eastern side of the River Tay and opened a temporary station at Barnhill in May 1847 but it was not until March 1849 that they managed to cross the river to a station at Princess Street on the west bank of the river. Originally fitted with a swinging section to facilitate river traffic, this was later replaced as seen in the photograph. An example of the earlier constructed class members, No. 62706 entered service from Darlington Works late in 1927 and would be withdrawn 31 years later in 1958 whilst based at Thornton Junction shed. (WS14)

Above: Saturday 12 March 1955. Seen arriving at Gleneagles station with the 11.35am working from Dundee West to Glasgow Buchanan Street is ex-LMS Class 5 4-6-0 No. 45470. It is fitted with a miniature snow plough. Constructed at Crewe Works and entering service late in 1938 she would be withdrawn during 1964 having given only twenty-six years of service. Note the detail on the station name board, 'GLENEAGLES for AUCTERARDER WEST and junction for CRIEFF and COMRIE'. The former Caledonian Railway branch originally extended from Gleneagles to Crieff, Comrie and Lochearnhead making a junction with the Callander and Oban Railway at Balquhidder which was opened throughout during 1905. Closed to passenger traffic between Balquhidder and Comrie in 1951 the section between Comrie and Gleneagles finally closed in July 1964. (WS2746)

29

Opposite top: Saturday 21 May 1955. Waiting to depart from Hawick station at the head of the 4.32pm local to Hexham via the 'Border Counties' route is British Railways Standard Class 4 2-6-0 No. 76046. Constructed at Doncaster Works during 1955 and allocated to Gateshead shed, she would end her days based at Corkerhill shed in Glasgow and be withdrawn in 1967. The journey through the spectacular borders country route stretching from Riccarton Junction to Hexham via Reedsmouth will take about three and a half hours to complete. This passenger service would be withdrawn during October 1956. (WS3535)

Opposite bottom: Saturday 21 May 1955. Prior to the departure of the 6.29pm stopping service from Musselburgh to Edinburgh Waverley, the photographer has asked the driver of ex-LNER Class V3 2-6-2 tank No. 67668 to pose next to his charge. Constructed at Doncaster Works during 1938 as a V1 locomotive, she would be rebuilt in 1954 as a V3 version of the class. Initially allocated to Stratford shed, she would end her days based at St Margarets shed in Edinburgh and be withdrawn in 1962. (WS2517)

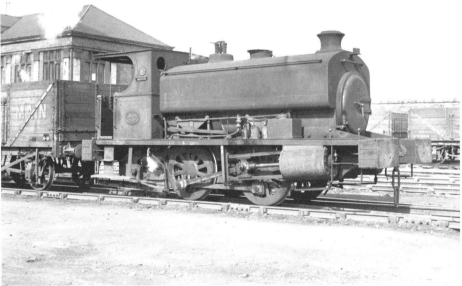

This page: Saturday 21 May 1955. Granton Gas Works lay close to the foreshore adjoining the harbour at Granton and was served by the ex-Caledonian Railway Granton branch. Opened in 1902 by the Edinburgh and Leith Corporation, the layout incorporated the works own passenger station which was opened in 1903 with services from Princes Street station carrying workers to and from the site. The station closed in 1942 and is now the only remaining structure on the former gas works site. In addition to the standard gauge sidings for the handling of coal and coke, the works operated a 2' gauge system to handle waste and by products.

This page, top: In the works yard is seen SGB No. 10 an 0-4-0 saddle tank constructed by Andrew Barclay during 1926 with their works number 1890. Moving into the preserved scene, she is currently operational and is based at the Fife Heritage Railway in Leven and carries the name *Forth*. (WS3739)

This page, bottom: Also seen in the works yard is SGB No. 7 an 0-4-0 saddle tank and another product of Barclay, works number 1036 of 1904. (WS3740)

Opposite top: Saturday 6 August 1955. Standing adjacent to the shed at Stirling is ex-CR Class 92 (LMS Class 2P) 0-4-4 tank No. 55126 bearing the correct 63B shed code for this date. Constructed at St Rollox Works during 1897 she would give 64 years of service being withdrawn in 1961. The smokebox door is held closed by a single handle on a thread supplemented by clamps around the perimeter. A number of ex-Caley tank engines utilized this method, (WS2174)

Opposite bottom: Saturday 6 August 1955. Sitting outside the entrance to the shed at Stirling Shore Street, is ex-CR Class 72 (LMS Class 3P) 4-4-0 No. 54504. This William Pickersgill design of superheated boilered locomotives for the Caledonian Railway were introduced during 1916 with a total of 48 examples being constructed in batches up to 1922. In addition to St Rollox Works, examples from the NBL at both their Atlas and Hyde Park Works along with Armstrong Whitworth & Co, supplied the greater majority of the class numbers. No. 54504 entered service from the NBL in 1922 and was numbered 93 by the Caley, renumbered 14504 by the LMS she would give 37 years of service being withdrawn in 1959. (WS3315)

Above: Thursday 25 August 1955. Waiting to depart from Crieff station with the 5.24pm working to Gleneagles is ex-LMS Class 4F 0-6-0 No. 44193. One of 60 examples of the class constructed at St Rollox Works, she entered service during 1925 and would spend her working life based at Scottish sheds. Seen here bearing a 63A Perth shed code, she would end her days based at Motherwell and be withdrawn in 1962. The Crieff to Gleneagles branch would close to traffic during July 1964. (WS3672)

Opposite: Wednesday 31 August 1955. Ex-LNER Class A2 4-6-2 No. 60525 *A. H. Peppercorn* was the only member of the class to enter service from Doncaster Works prior to nationalisation in December 1947 and was originally numbered 525 by the LNER. Allocated to Ferryhill shed in Aberdeen during 1949 she remained based there until withdrawn in 1963. She is seen here waiting to depart from Aberdeen station at the head of the 5.18pm express to Edinburgh Waverley. The 'E' prefix to the number of the first vehicle indicates it was allocated to the Eastern Region. (WS48)

Above: Monday 29 August 1955. Undertaking the task for which it was designed, ex-NBR Class G (LNER Class Y9) 0-4-0 saddle tank No. 68102, together with its wooden coal tender, is shunting in Leith Docks. Constructed at Cowlairs Works in 1891 and numbered 227 and later 1089 by the NBR, she would become No. 10089 and later 8102 with the LNER. This example does not have a spark arrestor whilst the (wooden) dumb buffers will be noted. Originating in a design by Neilson & Co., two locomotives designated Class G by the NBR were purchased by them in 1882, the basic design was subsequently perpetuated at Cowlairs Works with a total of 35 further examples built between 1887 and 1899. All 35 engines were rebuilt over a period of many years with new boilers, altered and enlarged cabs and buffers. Classified Y9 by the LNER, 33 of the class passed to British Railways and one No. 68095 reached preservation. It can be seen at the SRPS base at Bo'ness. No. 68102 was not so fortunate, being withdrawn during 1958 having given 67 years of service. (WS2231)

Above: Saturday 3 September 1955. Parked in the yard at Hawick shed undergoing some maintenance is ex-NBR Class C (LNER Class J36) 0-6-0 No. 65331. A tender cab is fitted which would afford the crew some protection in inclement weather or when running tender-first. A product of Cowlairs Works during 1900 and give 63 years of service being withdrawn in 1963. (WS3077)

Opposite bottom: Saturday 3 December 1955. At Forfar shed ex-CR Class 439 (LMS Class 2P) 0-4-4 tank No. 55200 is taking water on board before moving forward to take coal. Constructed at St Rollox Works in 1909 she would be allocated to sheds as far afield as Oban and Forfar spending the last years of her working life based at Perth shed and being withdrawn from service during 1961. This design of 0-4-4 tank locomotive had its origins with Dugald Drummond and his Class 171 locomotives whose first examples were constructed at St Rollox Works during 1884. John Lambie and John McIntosh continued construction with slight variations from 1895 until 1914 by which time a total of 146 had entered service. William Pickersgill had a further 14 constructed and even the LMS saw their worth and had a further ten built in 1925. Only one example made it into the preservation scene with CR No. 419 being based at the SRPS site at Bo'ness. (WS2198)

Above: Saturday 3 September 1955. Arriving at Galashiels station at the head of the 2.33pm Edinburgh Waverley to Carlisle working is ex-LNER Class A3 4-6-2 No. 60035 *Windsor Lad*. Constructed at Doncaster Works during 1934 and allocated new to Haymarket shed in Edinburgh, she was named after that years Derby and St Leger races winner. She would receive a double chimney in 1959 and be withdrawn from service during 1961. Note the porter waiting on the platform with a barrow loaded with mailbags ready to load on the train. (WS3079)

Opposite top: Saturday 31 December 1955. The final day of this year sees ex-LMS Class 4P 'Compound' 4-4-0 No. 40938 carrying out shunting duties in Dundee West station sidings. Constructed at Derby Works during 1932 she would be allocated to Scottish sheds, being finally based at Perth from where she was withdrawn after only 24 years of service in 1956. (WS600)

Opposite bottom: Saturday 5 May 1956. This last day of passenger services on the branch between Polmont and Bo'ness saw Class 4MT 2-6-0 No. 43141 working the 1.57pm service from Bo'ness consisting of four coaches. With only four daily return services the branch to the port was poorly served with the normal consist being a Class C16 and two coaches. The River Forth and Bo'ness Harbour are in the background, although this scene was swept away later in consequence of land reclamation on the foreshore. No. 43141 was a post-nationalisation product of Doncaster Works during 1951 that would be allocated new to Polmont shed and end her days at Normanton shed, being withdrawn in 1966. (WS3586)

Above: Monday 16 July 1956. Ex-CR Class 711 (LMS Class 2F) 0-6-0 No. 57396 is seen entering Muthill station with the afternoon goods train from Crieff to Stirling. Entering service from St Rollox Works during 1895 she would, by 1953 be allocated to Stirling shed from where she would be withdrawn in 1958. (WS3677)

Above: Saturday 2 February 1957. Arriving at Gorgie station at the head of the 11.51am football special from Partick Hill in Glasgow, is ex-LNER Class B1 4-6-0 No. 61117 bearing a 65C Parkhead shed code. Carrying Rangers football club supporters to a Scottish Cup Fifth Round match against Heart of Midlothian at Tynecastle, they will come away as victors their team having scored four goals without reply from Hearts. No. 61117 was the product of the NBL in Glasgow in 1947 that would spend time allocated to Eastfield and Parkhead sheds in Glasgow before ending her days at St Margarets in Edinburgh being withdrawn during 1964. (WS2217)

Opposite top: Saturday 2 February 1957. This day also saw the Five Nations Rugby match between Scotland and Wales taking place at Murrayfield in Edinburgh. Several special trains were worked between Princes Street and Murrayfield to carry fans to the stadium at Murrayfield. Seen here is ex-NBR Class B (LNER Class J37) 0-6-0 No. 64574 arriving at Murrayfield with the 1.51pm special. Constructed at Cowlairs Works during 1918 she would give 44 years service being withdrawn in 1962. The result of the rugby match was Scotland nine points, Wales six points. (WS2204)

Opposite bottom: Saturday 30 March 1957. Standing in Haymarket shed yard is ex-LNER Class D49/2 4-4-0 No 62743 *The Cleveland* bearing the correct 64B shed code. The small figure of a fox applied above the nameplate was fitted to all the 'Hunt' series of locomotive names. Constructed at Darlington Works during 1932, this photograph clearly shows the Lentz Rotary Cam Valve Gear fitted to the part 2 examples of the class. Initially allocated to Gateshead shed she was transferred to Haymarket during 1951 from where she would be withdrawn from service in 1960. (WS22)

Opposite top: Monday 22 April 1957. The time is 3.05pm and at Largo station the 2.30pm Crail to Thornton Junction passenger train is crossing with the 2.39pm Thornton Junction to Crail passenger working. At the head of the 'up' train is ex-NBR Class J 'Superheated Scott' (LNER Class D30) 4-4-0 No. 62418 *The Pirate*. Constructed at Cowlairs Works during 1914 by this time she was based at Thornton Junction but would be withdrawn from service in 1959. The locomotive was named after the Sir Walter Scott novel 'The Pirate' which was published in 1822. (WS3621)

Opposite bottom: Monday 22 April 1957. Kilconquhar station was originally the terminus for the East of Fife Railway that opened between Leven and Kilconquhar in August 1857. The extension eastward was opened by the Leven and East of Fife Railway during September 1863 when it reached Anstruther. The last sections between Anstruther and St Andrews were finally opened in June 1887. The bulk of the line was closed to passenger traffic in September 1965 with the remainder closing in October 1969. Ex-LNER Class B1 4-6-0 No. 61118 is seen entering Kilconquhar station at the head of the 2.10pm working from Dundee Tay Bridge to Edinburgh Waverley via the Fife Coast Line. Allocated to 62A Thornton Junction shed she was constructed by the NBL in 1947 and would be withdrawn during 1964. (WS2796)

Above: Saturday 18 May 1957. Certainly not the most handsome of locomotives, the former LMS 2-6-0s which became known as 'Crabs' to railwaymen, were introduced during 1926, the design being attributed to the ex-Lancashire and Yorkshire Railway Locomotive Superintendent George Hughes. Primarily designed to handle goods traffic, ten examples of the class were allocated to ex-Highland Railway territory during 1928 but were originally restricted to working the main line between Perth and Inverness via Slochd. Seen here at Perth Princes Street station working the 5.45pm Perth to Dundee West service is No. 42800. A product of Crewe Works during 1928 she would be withdrawn from service in 1965. (WS506)

Opposite top: Monday 27 May 1957. Working as Stirling station pilot on this day is ex-CR Class 439 (LMS Class 2P) 0-4-4 tank No. 55195, she is fitted with a chimney that might well be described as 'minimalist'. . Allocated to Stirling shed, 63B since 1955, she was constructed at St Rollox Works during 1909 and would be withdrawn in 1961. (WS713)

Opposite bottom: Saturday 12 October 1957. In clean condition ex-NBR Class C (LNER Class J36) 0-6-0 No. 65243 is standing in the yard at Haymarket shed. Constructed by Neilson & Co during 1891 and numbered 673 by the NBR, she would be rebuilt in the form seen here in 1915. Requisitioned by the War Department in 1917 she served in France with 24 of her classmates and was returned to the NBR in 1919. Later given the name *Maude* after Lieutenant General Sir Frederick Stanley Maude who served on both the Western Front and in Mesopotamia during the First World War. She is seen here without the name which would be re-applied at a later date. Withdrawn from service in 1966 she was purchased by the Scottish Railway Preservation Society and is currently on display at their museum at Bo'ness. (WS43)

Above: Tuesday 18 March 1958. Working hard near Larbert with the 2.00pm Dundee West to Glasgow Buchanan Street express is ex-LNER Class B1 4-6-0 No. 61221 *Sir Alexander Erskine-Hill*. Named after the first Baronet Quothquan of Lanark, the former Member of Parliament for Edinburgh North, she entered service from the NBL late in 1947 and was initially allocated to Carlisle Canal shed. Re-allocated later that year to Haymarket in Edinburgh she would end her days based at Dundee Tay Bridge shed and be withdrawn during 1965. (WS10)

Opposite: Saturday 22 March 1958. Normally a turn for a B1 Class locomotive, the 12.48pm Leven to Edinburgh Waverley stopper is in the hands of a sparklingly clean Class A1 4-6-2 No. 60160 *Auld Reekie* as it enters Cameron Bridge station. Possibly fresh from overhaul this could well be a running-in turn for the engine. Constructed at Doncaster Works during 1949 she would be allocated new to Haymarket shed in Edinburgh. After a spell based at Polmadie in Glasgow she would end her days at St Margarets in Edinburgh and be withdrawn in 1963. Note the Distillers Company Ltd (DCL) private owner grain wagons in the adjoining siding which served the large distillery at Cameron Bridge. (WS3604)

Above: Saturday 22 March 1958. Designed as a lighter version of the Class 7P6F 'Britannia' Pacific locomotives, the Class 6P5F 'Clan' class had an original construction order for 25 examples which was quickly reduced to only ten all of which entered service from Crewe Works during 1951 and 1952. Initially intended to be allocated to work the ex-Highland Railway route to Inverness they were instead allocated to Polmadie in Glasgow (66A) and Kingmoor in Carlisle (12A). Seen here entering Sinclairtown station working the 10.40am Edinburgh Waverley to Dundee Tay Bridge stopper is the first of the class No. 72000 *Clan Buchanan*. Entering service in December 1951 she acquired her name on 15 January 1952 with a ceremony at Glasgow Central station but would only give 11 years of service before ceasing work during 1962. (WS520)

Opposite top: Saturday 22 March 1958. At the East Wemyss shed of the Wemyss Private Railway, Andrew Barclay constructed 0-6-0 tank No. 19 is standing in the yard. Constructed during 1939 and given the works number 2067, she was an example of the very powerful 0-6-0 tanks produced by that company. In the shed in the background, the bunker of sister locomotive No. 20 can be seen. She was purchased by the Scottish Railway Preservation Society after withdrawal in 1970 and is currently under overhaul at its base in Bo'ness. Another member of the class, Wemyss Private Railway No. 17, also managed to reach the preservation scene and is currently based at the Speyside Railway at Aviemore. (WS3721)

Opposite bottom: Saturday 5 April 1958. Acting as Aberdeen station south end No. 1 pilot on this day was ex-NBR Class A (LNER Class N15/2) 0-6-2 tank No. 69129. Constructed by the NBL in 1910 she would be withdrawn from service eight months later during December 1958. (WS2308)

Above: Saturday 5 July 1958. This excellent view at the western end of Waverley station in Edinburgh shows ex-LNER three cylinder Class V2 2-6-2 No. 60804 departing with a working to Aberdeen. One of the early Doncaster constructed examples of this class, she entered service in 1936 being allocated to Dundee Tay Bridge shed from where she would be withdrawn in 1963. (WS67)

Above: Saturday 9 August 1958. The 5.40pm local working from Dunfermline Lower to Thornton Junction via Cowdenbeath has just arrived at its destination and the passengers are alighting. In charge of this two coach working is ex-NBR Class B (LNER Class J37) 0-6-0 No. 64635. Constructed at Cowlairs Works during 1910 she would initially be withdrawn in 1962 but would be returned to service for a short period and be finally withdrawn during 1963. (WS245)

Opposite top: Saturday 20 September 1958. Passing the long closed Esplanade station which lay at the northern end of the Tay Bridge in Dundee, ex-LNER Class V2 2-6-2 No. 60973 is hauling a set of empty coaching stock. One of the last examples of the class to be constructed, she entered service during 1943 from Darlington Works but would only remain working for 23 years being withdrawn in 1966. (WS75)

Opposite bottom: Saturday 20 September 1958. Seen departing from Dundee Tay Bridge station with the 5.25pm local to St Andrews is ex-LNER Class J39 0-6-0 No. 64792 bearing a 62B Dundee shed code. Constructed at Darlington Works during 1929 and numbered 2739 by the LNER she was allocated new to Carlisle Canal shed. She would be transferred to Dundee Tay Bridge shed in 1943 and re-allocated to Thornton Junction in 1959 from where she would be withdrawn in 1962. (WS251)

With the completion of the Class J38 locomotives during 1926, all of which were allocated to Scottish sheds to handle the heavy coal traffic, primarily in the Fife area, construction commenced on the very similar Class J39 goods locomotives. The main difference in the two classes was the use of larger diameter driving wheels of 5' 2" on the J39 instead of the 4' 8" on the J38s. Allocation to Scottish sheds varied throughout their lifetime with examples based at St Margarets and Dalry Road in Edinburgh, Eastfield and Parkhead in Glasgow and Dundee Tay Bridge and Ferryhill in Aberdeen.

Above: Saturday 20 September 1958. On the same day another Class J39 is seen here standing in the yard at Dundee Tay Bridge shed. Again bearing the correct 62B shed code No. 64786 was a further example of a Darlington Works constructed locomotive entering service in 1929. Numbered 2733 by the LNER and allocated new to Parkhead shed in Glasgow she would move to Dundee Tay Bridge during 1947 and be withdrawn during 1962. (WS2194)

Opposite top: Saturday 20 September 1958. In Dundee Tay Bridge shed yard with a group of enginemen standing in the background, the photographer has captured the well balanced lines of ex-NBR Class L (LNER Class C16) 4-4-2 tank No. 67486. Designed by William Reid to undertake the heavy suburban duties around Glasgow and Edinburgh, No. 67486 had been constructed by the NBL during 1915 and numbered 442 by the NBR. Later becoming 9442 and 7486 with the LNER she would be transferred to Dundee in the early 1930s and be withdrawn from service in 1960. (WS2396)

Opposite bottom: Saturday 20 September 1958. In Dundee West shed yard, ex-NBR Class D (LNER Class J83) 0-6-0 tank No. 68452 had technically been withdrawn from service three months earlier. Designed by Matthew Holmes to handle goods traffic, members of the class could also be found being utilised on short branch passenger duties around Edinburgh. No 68452 was the product of Neilson, Reid & Co in 1901 that would give 57 years of service, (WS2202)

Above: Saturday 20 September 1958. Also seen standing in Dundee West shed yard is ex-NBR Class K (LNER Class D34) 'Glen' 4-4-0 No. 62485 *Glen Murr*an. Constructed at Cowlairs Works during 1919 she would be withdrawn from service in 1960. Dundee Tay Bridge shed was nearby and as a result the yard at Dundee West had become a storage area for steam. Dundee West officially closed in 1958 although the facility was re-opened as a DMU maintenance depot two years later. One of the new diesel sets may be seen behind No. 62485. (WS2398)

Opposite top: Saturday 15 November 1958. Pausing at Fountainhall station at the head of the 12.52pm Edinburgh Waverley to Hawick service is Class B1 4-6-0 No. 61307. Constructed by the NBL during 1948 she was allocated new to Kittybrewster shed in Aberdeen and became something of a wanderer being subsequently allocated to Keith, Bathgate, Thornton Junction and finally St Margarets shed in Edinburgh from where she was withdrawn in 1966. The crowd of enthusiasts on the platform are gathered to witness the last passenger train to work on the Lauder branch which was organised by the Branch Line Society and was hauled by BR Standard Class 2 2-6-0 No. 78049. The Lauder Light Railway had opened in July 1901 but passenger returns were so low that the service closed during September 1932. Goods services continued until September 1958 with this special last train seeing the complete closure of the line. (WS220)

Opposite bottom: Saturday 3 January 1959. Ex-LNER Class B1 4-6-0 No. 61180 has just arrived at Dundee East station at the head of the 1.30pm 'local' working from Arbroath. One of a batch of 50 examples of the class constructed by the Vulcan Foundry during 1947 for the LNER she would be numbered 1180 by them and allocated new to Eastfield shed in Glasgow. Spending time allocated to Dunfermline and Ferryhill in Aberdeen she would end her days based at Dundee Tay Bridge shed and be withdrawn during 1967. (WS2190)

Opposite top: Monday 30 March 1959. With steam to spare, ex-CR Class 294 (LMS Class 2F) 0-6-0 No. 57257 is waiting to depart from Doune station with a Callander to Stirling goods train. A real veteran, she had been constructed by Neilson Reid & Co during 1883 and would not be withdrawn from service until 1961 having given 77 years of service. (WS3453)

Opposite bottom: Saturday 4 April 1959. This day saw the running of the Branch Line Society 'Scott Country Rail Tour' taking in both the Selkirk and Jedburgh branches. Motive power was ex-NBR Class K (LNER Class D34) 'Glen' 4-4-0 No. 62471 *Glen Falloch* suitably turned out by the St Margarets shed staff. Seen here at Earlston crossing on the line between Greenlaw and St Boswells, the young spectators appear to be enjoying its passing. Constructed at Cowlairs Works in 1913 she would be withdrawn from service the following year, 1960. (WS187)

Top: Saturday 11 April 1959. With the Ochil Hills in the background, the 2.45pm Saturday only Stirling to Perth via Alloa and Kinross Junction working has paused at Dollar station with its three coach train. In charge is ex-LMS Class 4P 2-6-4 tank No. 42693. A product of Derby Works in 1945 she would spend time allocated to Polmadie in Glasgow, Dundee Tay Bridge and Stirling sheds before ending her days undertaking banking duties at Beattock and be withdrawn during 1966. Dollar station was opened by the NBR in May 1869 as part of the Devon Valley route between Stirling and Perth and which joined the Edinburgh to Perth line at Kinross Junction. Opened throughout in 1871 the section between Tillicoutry and Crook of Devon basically followed the beautifully scenic valley of the River Devon. The section from Alloa to Kinross was closed to passengers in June 1964 with the coal mine at Dollar retaining its connection until it too closed in 1973. (WS3536)

Opposite: Saturday 4 July 1959. Seen working as the Thornton Junction station pilot is ex-LNER Class D49/1 4-4-0 No. 62728 *Cheshire*. Entering service from Darlington Works in 1929 her final allocation would be Thornton Junction from where she was withdrawn during October 1959. (WS3491)

Above: Saturday 4 July 1959. At Dundee Tay Bridge station ex-LNER Class A2/1 4-6-2 No. 60509 *Waverley* is working the 5.17pm Aberdeen to Edinburgh express. It has a booked ten minute stop-over and the crew are taking the opportunity to fill the tender with water. This class of only four examples of the Edward Thompson designed development of the Class V2 locomotives were constructed at Darlington Works and entered service in 1944 and 1945. No. 60509 was a 1944 example that would be allocated to Haymarket shed in Edinburgh for much of her working life being withdrawn during August 1960. She is being passed by shed-mate ex-LNER Class A3 4-6-2 No. 60087 *Blenheim* whose lamps indicate she is either working empty coaching stock or a parcels train. Constructed at Doncaster Works during 1930 she had been fitted with a double chimney in 1958 and would acquire German trough style smoke deflectors during 1962. She had spent much of her life working out of Haymarket shed in Edinburgh but would be withdrawn from service during 1963 whilst based at St Margarets shed in Edinburgh. (WS2191)

Above: Saturday 4 July 1959. The ex-NBR Class B and S locomotives (LNER Class J37) were the final development of the 0-6-0 wheelbase variety designed by William Reid for the NBR to handle the massive amounts of coal traffic coming out of their territory. No 64544 is seen shunting in Montrose goods yard, constructed by Cowlairs Works and entering service during 1914 she would be numbered 260 by the NBR. Later numbered 9260 and finally 4544 by the LNER she would spend much of the 1950s based at Dundee Tay Bridge shed and be withdrawn after 47 years service in 1962. (WS2193)

Opposite top: Saturday 4 July 1959. Ex-LNER Class V2 2-6-2 No. 60873 *Coldstreamer* is restarting the 3.10pm Saturdays only Aberdeen to Edinburgh Waverley express from Montrose station. Entering service from Doncaster Works during May 1939 she was named during a ceremony at Kings Cross station on 20 June 1939. Initially allocated to Kings Cross shed in London, she would be transferred to St Margarets in Edinburgh during 1951 and be withdrawn from service during 1962. (WS3548)

Opposite bottom: Saturday 4 July 1959. Ex-LNER Class V2 2-6-2 No. 60965 is seen passing Montrose North signal box at the head of the 3.40pm Aberdeen to Edinburgh Waverley express which will stop at Montrose station having taken almost exactly an hour to complete the 40 miles from Aberdeen. Constructed at Darlington Works during 1943 she would be allocated to St Margarets shed in Edinburgh from 1952 and be withdrawn late in 1962 having given less that 20 years of service. (WS3546)

Above: Saturday 18 July 1959. Preparing to depart from Eyemouth station with the 5.10pm working to Burnmouth is ex-LNER Class J39 0-6-0 No. 64843 bearing a 52D Tweedmouth shed code. Constructed at Darlington Works in 1932 she would be withdrawn from service thirty years later in 1962. The three mile Eyemouth branch was opened by the Eyemouth Railway in April 1891 but worked from the outset by the NBR. The branch traffic consisted mostly of fish from the large fishing fleet in the harbour that had been extended and deepened between 1885 and 1887. The line was closed to all traffic in February 1962. (WS2518)

Opposite top: Monday 20 July 1959. Pausing at Dalmeny station at the head of the 5.35pm Edinburgh Waverley to Dundee local working is ex-LNER Class V2 2-6-2 No. 60827. This train stopped at all stations to Dundee Tay Bridge and took approximately two and a half hours to complete the journey. The servicemen seen are a reminder that in the days of National Service it was commonplace to see men in uniform at stations and in the streets. The locomotive was a 1938 Darlington Works example of the class that was initially allocated to New England shed. She would find her way to Scottish sheds from 1945 and be withdrawn from service in 1962 whilst based at St Margarets shed in Edinburgh. (WS71)

Opposite bottom: Monday 20 July 1959. The photographer has noted the unusual choice of locomotive for this working, the 3.36pm Thornton Junction to Glasgow Queen Street local which is seen here at Dalmeny Junction being hauled by ex-LMS Class 6P5F 4-6-0 'Jubilee' No. 45724 *Warspite.* Built at Crewe Works during 1936 she would be allocated to Carlisle Kingmoor at the date of this photograph but would end her working life based at Nuneaton shed from where she would be withdrawn in 1962. (WS2490)

Above: Saturday 25 July 1959. Departing from Elie station at the head of the 12.52pm Crail to Edinburgh Waverley working is ex-NBR Class K (LNER Class D34) 'Glen' 4-4-0 No. 62478 *Glen Quoich*. Constructed at Cowlairs Works in 1917 she would be withdrawn during December 1959. The rudimentary chock on the rail from the siding may be noted. (WS3623)

Opposite top: Saturday 25 July 1959. Standing in the yard at Thornton Junction shed is ex-NBR Class K (LNER Class D34) 4-4-0 No. 62475 *Glen Beasdale*. Entering service from Cowlairs Works during 1913 she had been withdrawn during the month prior to this photograph, June 1959. (WS177)

The William Reid design of 'Superheated Intermediate' or 'Glen' Class K 4-4-0 type for the NBR were introduced during 1913 with a total of 32 entering service from Cowlairs Works, the last in 1920. With a reputation as efficient, reliable, good steamers the bulk of the class were kept at Eastfield in Glasgow working on the West Highland line to Fort William and its extension to Mallaig. They continued handling traffic on these routes, very often double headed, well into the 1940s. Other members of the type were allocated to St Margarets in Edinburgh and could be seen working to Glasgow, Dundee and the Fife coast.

Opposite bottom: Saturday 25 July 1959. In good clean condition ex-NBR Class C (LNER Class J36) 0-6-0 No. 65218 is standing in the yard at Thornton Junction shed. Constructed at Cowlairs Works during 1890 she would be numbered 632 by the NBR and become No. 9632 and later 5218 with the LNER. Rebuilt in the form seen here in 1914 she would give 72 years of service being withdrawn during 1962. (WS44)

Above: Friday 28 August 1959. Seen arriving at Rothes station is the 12.45pm Inverness to Aberdeen working which after Elgin would travel via Dufftown and Keith Town, the whole journey taking a few minutes short of four hours to complete. In charge is BR Standard Class 4 2-6-4 tank No. 80004. A product of Derby Works in 1952 she was allocated new to Kittybrewster shed in Aberdeen and would end her days based at Corkerhill in Glasgow being withdrawn during 1967. Rothes was the home to four distilleries which in turn generated a large amount of traffic for its goods yard. (WS3861)

Opposite top: Friday 28 August 1959. Seen pausing at Nairn station is the 10.10am Inverness to Glasgow Buchanan Street via Forres working. In charge is BR Standard Class 4 2-6-0 No. 76104 which is piloting Class 5 4-6-0 No. 44698. The Standard was a product of Doncaster Works entering service during 1957, which was then allocated to Kittybrewster in Aberdeen, She would end her days based at Polmadie in Glasgow and be withdrawn less than ten years later in 1967. The 'Black 5' had come out of Horwich Works in 1948 and she would be based at Perth shed for her entire working life, being withdrawn during 1966. (WS3864)

Opposite bottom: Friday 28 August 1959. BR Standard Class 4 2-6-4 tank No. 80021 is working the coast line section of the 3.40pm Aberdeen to Elgin working and is seen at Port Gordon station. Constructed at Brighton Works in 1951 she was allocated new to Kittybrewster shed in Aberdeen but would end her days based at Corkerhill in Glasgow and be withdrawn during 1964. (WS2756)

Opposite: Friday 28 August 1959. At Elgin shed ex-GNR Class H3 (LNER Class K2) 2-6-0 No. 61782 *Loch Eil* is moving on to the turntable. A product of Kitson & Co during 1921 she would be named in 1933 and transferred to Keith shed during 1954 and would give 39 years of service being withdrawn in 1960. In the background is 0-4-0 diesel shunter No. D2414. (WS3808)

Above: Saturday 29 August 1959. This day saw the running of the Stephenson Locomotive Society Scottish Area 'Festival Special' which visited several branches in the Edinburgh area. From Waverley station it worked to Glencorse, Polton and Penicuik returning via the Edinburgh suburban line to Waverley station. Power was provided throughout by the preserved ex-NBR Class K (LNER Class D34) 'Glen' 4-4-0 No. 256 *Glen Douglas*. She is seen here pausing at Gilmerton station on the Glencorse branch with the winding gear of Gilmerton colliery, which was closed in 1961, in the background. The three branch lines mentioned generated much traffic for the railway with the Glencorse branch serving a number of collieries as well as the Penicuik gas works which stood at the top of the town. The short Polton branch served three paper mills at Polton all with their own sidings and the branch to Penicuik, which followed the valley of the North Esk river also served a number of paper mills also having their own private sidinsg. The Valleyfield Mill at Peniculk which was owned by Messrs. Cowans, provided its own locomotive to shunt their sidings. This was a Hawthorn, Leslie 0-4-0 saddle tank which has managed to survive and reach the preservation scene. It is currently in the possession of the Aln valley Railway at Alnwick. (WS377)

Opposite top: Saturday 7 November 1959. Making a spirited departure from Waverley station at the head of the 12.15pm Saturday only working to Thornton Junction via Cowdenbeath, is Class B1 4-6-0 No. 61403 bearing a 62A Thornton Junction shed code. A post nationalisation example of the class from Darlington Works during 1950, she would spend her entire working life based at Scottish sheds and be withdrawn after only 16 years of service in 1966. (WS3927)

Opposite bottom: Saturday 7 November 1959. In ex-works condition ex-LNER Class B1 4-6-0 No. 61148 is seen departing from Waverley station at the head of the 12.30pm stopper to Dysart. Constructed by the Vulcan Foundry in 1947 she was allocated new to Kittybrewster shed in Aberdeen and by the date of this photograph was based at Thornton Junction shed from where she was withdrawn during 1966. (WS3928)

Above: Saturday 7 November 1959. Ex-LNER Class V3 2-6-2 tank No. 67615 is seen departing from Edinburgh Waverley station with the 12.35pm working to Corstorphine which lay in the western suburbs of Edinburgh. Constructed at Doncaster Works during 1931 as a Class V1 locomotive, she would be rebuilt in 1953 as a V3 version of the class. She appears to have been allocated to Haymarket shed in Edinburgh for her entire working life and be withdrawn during 1962. In the background is a Swindon built DMU set. (WS3929)

Above: Saturday 7 November 1959. Seen accelerating away from Newhaven station past an old CR lower quadrant signal, ex-LNER Class J39 0-6-0 No. 64986 is at the head of the 2.10pm Leith North to Princes Street station working. Constructed at Darlington Works during 1941 she would be allocated new to St Margarets in Edinburgh and by the date of this photograph had crossed the city to be based at the ex-Caley shed at Dalry Road. She would be withdrawn from service in 1962. (WS3931)

Opposite top: Saturday 7 November 1959. At Seafield shed yard in Edinburgh, close to Leith Docks, ex-NBR Class B (LNER Class J35) 0-6-0 No. 64532 is standing at the head of a row of locomotives. She is going through a disposal procedure with the fire having just been cleaned and the smoke box cleared of char. Constructed at Cowlairs Works in 1913 with a saturated boiler she would be rebuilt during 1934 with a superheating boiler and be withdrawn whilst based at St Margarets shed in Edinburgh during 1961. (WS3936)

Opposite bottom: Saturday 2 January 1960. The 12.10pm Perth to London Euston express is seen here passing Gleneagles station with ex-LMS Class 5 4-6-0 No. 44903 piloting ex-LMS Class 6P5F 'Jubilee' 4-6-0 No. 45742 *Connaught*. The 'Black 5' entered service from Crewe Works during 1945 and would be withdrawn in 1968 whilst the 'Jubilee' was the last member of the class to enter service, coming out of Crewe Works in December 1936. She would be withdrawn in 1965. The station retains is grandiose building to this day. (WS4003)

Above: Saturday 7 May 1960. Standing in Polmont shed yard in a rather grimy state is ex-NBR Class C (LNER Class J36) 0-6-0 No. 65306. A product of Cowlairs Works during 1899 she would be numbered 748 by the NBR and later 9748 and finally 5306 by the LNER. She would be rebuilt in the form seen here during 1921. With Polmont painted on her buffer beam and bearing a 64E shed code, she is at her allocated base but would be re-allocated to Grangemouth shed in 1961 and be withdrawn in 1962 having given 63 years of service. This class designed by Matthew Holmes and introduced during 1888 extended to 168 examples, the last appearing in 1900. All were rebuilt between 1913 and 1923 with larger boilers and Reid style larger more protective cabs replacing the original Holmes round topped variety. (WS4358)

Opposite top: Saturday 28 May 1960. Class A1 4-6-2 No. 60159 *Bonnie Dundee* is seen departing from Perth station at the head of the 8.20am Inverness to Edinburgh Waverley working and with a single fish van coupled immediately behind the tender. Named after the soubriquet of John Graham 7th Laird of Claverhouse, she entered service from Doncaster Works during 1949. Allocated new to Haymarket shed in Edinburgh she remained there until September 1963 when the shed was closed to steam locomotives. Re-allocated to St Margarets in Edinburgh she would be withdrawn the following month, October 1963. (WS4435)

Opposite bottom: Saturday 28 May 1960. The 12.10pm working to London Euston is seen departing from Perth station behind ex-LMS Class 6P5F 'Jubilee' 4-6-0 No. 45728 *Defiance* piloting class mate No 45718 *Dreadnought*. Both locomotives entered service from Crewe Works during 1936 and both would be withdrawn in 1962. (WS4436)

Opposite page: Between 12 and 17 June of 1960, the Stephenson Locomotive Society and the Railway Correspondence and Travel Society organised a joint 'Scottish Railtour' commencing at Edinburgh Waverley and finishing at Glasgow Central taking in much of the railway network in the east of Scotland behind a variety of preserved and service locomotives. This day saw the train visiting the Buchan and Aberdeenshire branches hauled by ex-GNoSR Class F (LNER Class D40) 4-4-0 No. 49 *Gordon Highlander*. Constructed by the NBL in 1920 and withdrawn during 1958 she entered Inverurie Works and was repainted in GNoSR livery and returned to service in July 1958 to haul special trains, she continued working specials throughout the 1960s and was finally withdrawn in 1966 and placed in the Riverside Museum in Glasgow. In the top view the engine is being manually turned on the table at Macduff whilst in the lower view the engine is departing from Inverurie station. (WS4545/4537)

Above: Monday 13 June 1960. Having worked 'light engine' along the Regent and Waterloo Quays in Aberdeen to reach the Waterloo goods yard, Andrew Barclay constructed 0-4-0 saddle tank, works number 2239 built in 1947, is preparing to work back to Aberdeen Gas Works with a train of coal tar tankers. Named *Mr Therm*, the name has almost completely disappeared from its tank-sides, after being withdrawn it would go on to static display in Seaton Park, Aberdeen. (WS4533)

Above: Monday 13 June 1960. Ex-LMS Class 2P 4-4-0 No. 40661 is standing adjacent to the works at Inverurie. Constructed at Derby Works during 1931 and numbered 661 by the LMS she would be allocated to Hurlford shed near Kilmarnock, she is still bearing the 67B shed code plate. Introduced in 1928 these Class 2P locomotives were a Henry Fowler development of the earlier Samuel Johnson Class 483 locomotives produced for the Midland Railway. A total of 138 examples were produced between 1928 and 1932, the bulk coming from Derby Works with 40 entering service from Crewe Works. No. 40661 would be withdrawn from service in November 1961. (WS4541)

Opposite top: Monday 13 June 1960. Seen on the turntable at Kittybrewster shed is ex-CR Class 652 (LMS Class 3F) 0-6-0 No. 57644 in ex-works condition and bearing a 67C Ayr shed code. Constructed at St Rollox Works during 1909 and numbered 328 by the CR she would become No. 17644 with the LMS and be withdrawn from service in 1962. With only 17 examples constructed this class was a modified version of the earlier McIntosh Class 812 design. (WS4566)

Opposite bottom: Tuesday 14 June 1960. Standing outside Keith shed is ex-CR Class 812 (LMS Class 3F) 0-6-0 No. 57591. Designed by John McIntosh and introduced during 1899 a total of 79 were constructed, the last appearing in 1900. Construction took place not only at St Rollox Works but by three outside manufacturers, Neilson Reid & Co, Sharp, Stewart & Co and Dubs & Co. No. 57591 was a product of Sharp, Stewart & Co during 1900 that would be numbered 853 by the Caley, later becoming No 17591 with the LMS. By the time of this photograph she was allocated to Aviemore shed and would end her days based at Dalry Road in Edinburgh and be withdrawn in 1961. (WS4569)

Opposite top: Tuesday 14 June 1960. Pausing at Alves station at the head of the 12.52pm Elgin to Inverness two coach local is ex-LMS Class 5 4-6-0 No. 45476. Constructed at Derby Works during 1943 she was allocated new to Inverness shed and is seen still bearing the 60A shed code plate. Transferred to Perth shed in August 1960 she would finally be based at Dalry Road in Edinburgh in 1961 and be withdrawn from service in 1964. Alves station was the junction for the branch to Burghead which had been opened by the Inverness and Aberdeen Joint Railway in December 1862 and extended to Hopeman in October 1893. Although the passenger service had been withdrawn in September 1931, goods traffic continued to serve the large maltings in the area with final closure of the line coming during 2017. Note the Manson tablet exchange mechanism at the end of the platform. (WS4578)

Opposite bottom: Tuesday 14 June 1960. In the morning of the same day as the previous photograph, No. 45476 is seen passing Elgin East 'box as it arrives at Elgin station with the coast worked portion of the 7.45am departure from Aberdeen. (WS4576)

Above: Tuesday 14 June 1960. The joint SLS/RCTS Scottish Rail Tour was visiting various lines and branches in the Moray, Nairn and Inverness-shire on this day. Commencing in Aberdeen the branches at Fochabers, Burghead and Fortrose would be visited with the day ending in Inverness. Motive power from Elgin to Burghead and Inverness would be ex-LMS Class 2P 4-4-0 No. 40663 which is seen here preparing to leave Alves, the junction for Burghead, with its five coach train. Constructed at Derby Works during 1931, she would be allocated to Kittybrewster shed in Aberdeen from 1954, she is carrying a 61A shed code, and would end her days at Ferryhill shed being withdrawn after 30 years of service in 1961. (WS4580)

Opposite top: Thursday 16 June 1960. By this date the SLS/RCTS joint Scottish Rail Tour was visiting lines and branches in Perthshire, Angus and Kincardine. Commencing in Perth the former Caledonian Railway branches at Alyth and Kirriemuir were traversed before proceeding to Forfar and on to the ex-CR goods yard at Montrose East. Motive power was ex-CR Class 711 (LMS Class 2F) 0-6-0 No. 57441 which is seen here waiting to depart from Kirriemuir. Originally designed by Dugald Drummond and introduced in 1883, construction of the class continued into the McIntosh era with this engine entering service from St Rollox Works during 1896. Numbered 572 by the Caley she became No. 17441 with the LMS. Allocated to Forfar shed, she is actually bearing a Perth 63A shed code and would give 65 years of service being withdrawn in 1961. (WS4641)

Opposite bottom: Thursday 16 June 1960. Class 2MT 2-6-0 No. 46464 is seen at Carmyllie station with the SLS/RCTS Scottish Rail Tour. Constructed at Crewe Works during 1950 she would be allocated new to St Margarets in Edinburgh and spend time allocated to Kittybrewster in Aberdeen and finally Dundee Tay Bridge from where she was withdrawn in 1966. Purchased privately and returned to steam during the 1970s she has worked at the Strathspey Railway but is currently under overhaul. No doubt the participants were delighted there were end windows in the leading vehicle. (WS4656)

Above: Thursday 16 June 1960. Preparing to depart from Perth station at the head of an evening trip to Dundee West at the head of the SLS/RCTS Scottish Rail Tour is the iconic Caley Single No. 123. Constructed by Neilson & Co for the Edinburgh International Exhibition of 1886, she was purchased later by the Caledonian Railway and used during the 1888 'Races to the North' working between Carlisle and Edinburgh. Withdrawn from service by the LMS during 1935 she was brought back into service by British Railways Scottish Region in 1958 and used on many special workings travelling as far south as the Bluebell Railway in Sussex. She is currently to be seen at the Riverside Museum in Glasgow. (WS4660)

Above: Thursday 16 June 1960. With a change of locomotive, the joint SLS/RCTS Scottish Rail Tour is now seen at the former Caledonian Railway goods yard at Montrose East station. Ex-NBR Class B (LNER Class J37) 0-6-0 No. 64615 would traverse the Inverbervie branch returning as far as Arbroath and Elliot Junction before another change of locomotive power took the train over the former Dundee and Arbroath Railway Carmyllie branch. Constructed by the NBL and entering service during 1920, No. 64615 would originally be numbered 46 by the NBR becoming No. 9046 and later No. 4615 with the LNER. Bearing a 62B Dundee Tay Bridge shed code she would be withdrawn in late 1962 but re-instated early in 1963 before finally being withdrawn in April 1963. (WS4644)

Opposite top: Saturday 6 August 1960. Waiting at Stirling station whilst parcels are dealt with from a northbound parcels train is BR Standard Class 6P5F 4-6-2 No. 72008 *Clan MacLeod*. Constructed at Crewe Works during 1952 she would be allocated to Kingmoor shed in Carlisle for her entire working life and be withdrawn in 1966. None of the ten examples of the class made it to the preservation scene but the Standard Steam Locomotive Company was set up to construct the eleventh member of the class to be numbered 72010 and named *Hengist*. (WS4857)

Opposite bottom: Saturday 25 March 1961. Designed by Nigel Gresley specifically to operate on the West Highland line, the five members of his three cylinder Class K4 2-6-0s were all initially allocated to Eastfield shed in Glasgow to work this route. Seen here in Thornton Junction shed yard is No. 61998 *MacLeod of MacLeod* named after the Chief of Clan MacLeod, she was initially named *Lord of Dunvegan* and was the last of the class to enter service in 1939 and would be withdrawn during 1961. (WS5214)

Above: Saturday 25 March 1961. Standing adjacent to the shed at Thornton Junction is ex-NBR Class D (LNER Class J83) 0-6-0 tank No. 68459. Constructed by Neilson, Reid & Co during 1901 she would give sixty years of service being withdrawn two months after this photograph in May 1961. The embellishment on the roof is one of the shed ventilators. (WS5215)

Opposite top: Saturday 20 May 1961. This day saw the running of the SLS Dundee Branch Angus Rail Tour which commenced at Glasgow Buchanan Street visiting Dundee West station and the Newtyle branch. Returning to Dundee it was worked through Tay Bridge station and traversed the branch from Broughty Ferry to Monikie. Returning to Dundee Tay Bridge it worked forward to Glasgow Queen Street via the Tay and Forth bridges. Motive power used for the Dundee West to Newtyle section was William Pickersgill designed ex-CR Class 72 4-4-0 No. 54500 which had been constructed by the NBL during 1922 and numbered 69 by the Caledonian. She is seen here at Dundee West station looking splendidly turned out for the occasion, she would be withdrawn less than a year later in 1962. (WS5356)

Opposite bottom: Saturday 1 July 1961. The 5.49pm local from Anstruther has arrived at Thornton Junction and passengers are alighting. In charge is ex-LNER Class J39 0-6-0 No. 64790 bearing a 62A Thornton Junction shed code. Built at Darlington Works during 1929 she would be numbered 2737 and later 4790 by the LNER. Allocated new to St Margarets in Edinburgh, she would spend time allocated to Carlisle Canal and Dundee Tay Bridge sheds before being based at Thornton Junction from 1959 from where she would be withdrawn in 1962. The J39s constituted one of the largest of the 0-6-0 goods locomotive classes produced by the LNER, a total of 289 examples were constructed of this Nigel Gresley design. The largest number entered service from Darlington Works between 1926 and 1941 with 28 examples being produced by Beyer, Peacock & Co during 1936 and 1937. Distributed widely throughout the LNER system, about 30 were allocated to Scottish sheds. (WS5541)

Above: Saturday 1 July 1961. Bearing a 64B Haymarket shed code, ex-LNER Class A3 4-6-2 No. 60098 *Spion Kop* has arrived at Thornton Junction station at the head of the 3.40pm Aberdeen to Edinburgh Waverley express. Constructed at Doncaster Works during 1929 and named after the 1920 Derby race winner, she had been allocated new to Doncaster shed but would become something of a wanderer, working from Haymarket in Edinburgh, Grantham and Gateshead sheds before ending her days at St Margarets shed in Edinburgh and being withdrawn from there in 1963. Introduced to the Great Northern Railway in 1922, Nigel Gresley's Class A1 locomotives would consist of a total of 52 examples that had been constructed by both Doncaster Works and the North British Locomotive Co in Glasgow, the last entering service in 1925. They were all rebuilt between 1927 and 1948 as Class A3 locomotives. Between 1928 and 1935 an additional 27 examples of the Class A3 were constructed at Doncaster Works. Designed to handle express passenger traffic throughout the LNER system they proved themselves to be reliable efficient workhorses with the last example No 60052 *Prince Palatine* being withdrawn for scrap in 1966. One example has survived, appropriately No 60103 *Flying Scotsman* at the time of writing operational and can be seen working specials throughout the U.K. (WS5542)

Opposite bottom; Monday 25 September 1961. With the retirement of Arthur Peppercorn from British Railways at the end of 1949, Robert Riddles was appointed as Director responsible for Mechanical and Electrical Engineering for the Railway Executive running the national railways. He instituted a range of designs for a series of locomotives that became known as the British Railways Standards with twelve classes envisaged ranging from a Pacific for express passenger work to a tank locomotive with a large route availability and a heavy goods locomotive. The first to appear were examples of the Class 7 Pacifics with No. 70000 *Britannia* exiting Crewe Works in January 1951 followed over a period of four years by a further 54 all coming from Crewe Works. The example seen here at Melrose station on the 'Waverley Route' is No. 70018 *Flying Dutchman* in charge of the 1.28pm Carlisle to Edinburgh Waverley working. Entering service during 1951 she would initially be allocated to the Western Region but end her days based at Carlisle sheds in 1966 being withdrawn during that year. (WS5718)

Above: Saturday 19 August 1961. In the beautiful Berwickshire countryside near Reston, Class A1 4-6-2 No. 60116 *Hal o' the Wynd* is at the head of the 2.00pm 'Heart of Midlothian' from Edinburgh Waverley to London Kings Cross express consisting of 13 coaches. Built at Doncaster Works in 1948 she would be allocated new to Heaton shed in Newcastle and be re-allocated to Tweedmouth during 1962 and Gateshead in 1964 being withdrawn from there during 1965 after having a short working life of only 17 years. Named during May 1951, the character Hal o' the Wynd was the nickname for the blacksmith Henry Gow who appears in the Sir Walter Scott title 'The Fair Maid of Perth' published in 1828. The name had also been used previously on the former North British Railway Class J (LNER Class D30) 4-4-0 No. 62417 which had been withdrawn from service during January 1951. When Arthur Peppercorn became CME of the LNER during 1946, that company was still suffering the effects of his predecessors design of Pacific locomotives which were prone to a number of failings. It is generally accepted that Peppercorns design for the Class A1 produced one of the most freely running steam locomotives constructed by the former LNER works. A total of 49 were produced during 1948 and 1949 with 23 coming out of Darlington Works and twenty-six from Doncaster Works. Unfortunately none survived into the preservation scene but the A1 Steam Locomotive Trust constructed the fiftieth member of the class and during 2008 No. 60163 *Tornado* came into service and has been working specials throughout the U.K. both on the main line and on the various heritage railways. (WS5643)

Opposite top: Saturday 30 September 1961. This day saw the running of the Branch Line Society 'The Pentland and Tinto Express' which commenced at Leith North station and proceeded to Carstairs and Symington before traversing the remains of the former Caledonian Railway Peebles branch as far as Broughton which had become the end of the line. Returning to Edinburgh, it used the Suburban Circle to reach Waverley station from Portobello Junction. Motive power used was ex-CR Class 19 (LMS Class 2P) 0-4-4 tank No. 55124 which had been suitably spruced up by the Dalry Road shed staff. Designed by John Lambie and constructed at St Rollox Works during 1895, she was the last of the class of ten examples to enter traffic. She is seen here waiting to depart from Broughton station and this would be her last duty as she was withdrawn from service immediately afterwards although it would be two years later before she was scrapped. (WS5733)

Opposite bottom: Saturday 3 February 1962. This day saw the running of the SLS Scottish Area 'Farewell to Peebles' tour commencing at Edinburgh Princes Street and working to Leith North before traversing the Edinburgh Suburban Circle to Niddrie, then on to Peebles via Leadburn. Return was made via Galashiels and the 'Waverley Route' to Waverley station in Edinburgh. Motive power for the first part of the tour was ex-CR Class 812 (LMS 3F) 0-6-0 No. 57550 seen here at Leith North station. Constructed at St Rollox Works during 1899 she would be withdrawn from service in December 1962. (WS5817)

Above: Thursday 24 May 1962. Occupied with shunting in the former Edinburgh and Dalkeith Railway goods yard at Dalkeith is ex-NBR Class B (LNER Class J35) 0-6-0 No. 64510, she is only six months away from being withdrawn in November of that year. Constructed by the NBL during 1910 she spent time based at Bathgate shed before ending her days allocated to St Margarets in Edinburgh. (WS5997)

Above: On Saturday 16 June 1962. Ex-LMS Class 5 4-6-0 No. 44978 is seen departing from Forres station at the head of the RCTS/SLS Scottish Rail Tour. She would work the train from Inverness as far as Aviemore before other locomotives would take over. Constructed at Crewe Works during 1946 she would be withdrawn from service only 19 years later in 1965. Modern traction is evident in the background in the shape of the Type 2 diesel. (WS6055)

Opposite top: Saturday 16 June 1962. On reaching Aviemore the 'Black 5' was replaced by ex-GNoSR No. 49 Gordon Highlander and ex-HR No. 103 who double headed the train to Keith Town station. Seen here at Ballindaloch the pair are preparing to depart for Keith Town. Both these locomotives are currently housed at the Riverside Museum in Glasgow. (WS6060)

Opposite bottom: Monday 16 July 1962. Overshadowed by the Edinburgh tenement buildings of Bonaly Road, Class 4P 2-6-4 tank No. 42172 is seen departing from Merchiston station with the 5.37pm working from Princes Street station to Lanark. Constructed at Derby Works during 1948 she would only give 14 years of service being withdrawn in December 1962. (WS6241)

Above: Saturday 25 August 1962. A clean J35 No. 64510 is seen here at St Leonard's goods depot in Edinburgh. Having propelled the four coach Stephenson locomotive Society 'Edinburgh and Dalkeith' Rail Tour up the 1 in 30 gradient from Duddingston goods yard to St Leonard's, she is waiting for passengers to board before making the return to Duddingston. (WS6292)

Opposite top: Saturday 17 November 1962. At Wormit station the 1.14pm Tayport to Dundee Tay Bridge working is in the hands of BR Standard Class 4 2-6-4 tank No. 80124. Constructed at Brighton Works during 1955 and allocated new to Dundee Tay Bridge shed, she would only give 11 years of service being withdrawn in 1966. (WS6445)

Opposite bottom: Wednesday 26 December 1962. At Queensferry Junction, Ratho, the daily 'Ferry Goods' working is being prepared to make its way to South Queensferry yard. The photographer has noted that it will proceed via Kirkliston yard and Dalmeny Naval Stores shunting as required. Ex-NBR Class C (LNER Class J36) 0-6-0 No. 65288 is bearing a 64A St Margarets shed code and was constructed at Cowlairs Works in 1897. She would give 70 years of service being withdrawn in June 1967 as one of the last main line steam locomotives working in Scotland. (WS6475)

Saturday 13 April 1963. The SLS/BLS 'Scottish Rambler' No. 2 Rail Tour had departed from Edinburgh Waverley and visited South Queensferry, Dunfermline, Cowdenbeath and had reached Thornton Junction where a change of locomotives was required for the next part of the journey to Markinch to visit the Leslie branch. Ex-NBR Class B (LNER Class J37) 0-6-0 No. 64618 of Thornton Shed is looking suitably spruced up for the task. Constructed by the NBL during 1920 she would be withdrawn in 1966. The branch from Markinch to Leslie had been opened during December 1861 and absorbed by the NBR in 1872. Primarily opened to tap into the paper manufacturing in the area, the two large mills served were the Auchmutty Mill just to the west of Markinch and the Fettykill Mill in Leslie, both of which had private sidings. The passenger service on the branch ceased in 1932 but goods continued until 1967 when the Fettykill Mill lost its service and 1992 when the Auchmutty Mill ceased taking supplies by rail. (WS6633)

Sunday 14 April 1963. On the following day the 'Scottish Rambler' No. 2 tour would depart from Edinburgh Waverley and reach the Border Country. Visiting Reston, Duns, Tweedmouth, Coldstream, Wooler, Roxburgh, Jedburgh, St Boswells, Greenlaw, and finally Hawick where locomotives would be changed. Motive power was Class B1 4-6-0 No. 61324 which is seen here during a pause at Duns station. Constructed by the NBL in 1948 she would be allocated new to Kittybrewster shed in Aberdeen but end her days based at St Margarets in Edinburgh and be withdrawn during 1965. The line between Reston and St Boswells had been opened by the NBR in three sections, firstly from Reston to Duns in August 1849, secondly from Duns to Earlston during November 1863 and finally from Earlston to meet the Waverley Route at Ravenswood Junction in October 1865. Promoted during the late 1840s as an alternative route by the NBR into Newcastle, it suffered from the opening of the Tweed Valley line giving direct access to the East Coast main line at Tweedmouth, south of the river Tweed. Following the serious floods of August 1948, the section between Greenlaw and Duns was closed to all traffic and in consequence, the Duns to Reston and the Greenlaw to St Boswells sections operated as separate branches. Passenger services between Greenlaw and St Boswells were withdrawn immediately, but Reston to Duns services carried on until withdrawn in September 1951. Goods services between Reston and Duns ceased in November 1966 and those from St Boswells to Greenlaw during July 1965. (WS6642)

Opposite top: Saturday 27 April 1963. Waiting to depart from Perth station with an express for Glasgow Buchanan Street is BR Standard Class 5 4-6-0 No. 73146. Constructed at Derby Works during 1957 she was one of the class fitted with British Caprotti valve gear and was one of the ten locomotives so fitted to be allocated to the Scottish Region. Destined to have a short working life of only ten years, No. 73146 was withdrawn in 1967. (WS6704)

Opposite bottom: Saturday 11 May 1963. The 5.11pm Edinburgh Waverley to Gorebridge is seen approaching that station behind BR Standard Class 4 2-6-4 tank No. 80055. Built at Derby Works during 1954 she would be allocated new to Polmadie shed in Glasgow and be transferred to St Margarets in Edinburgh in 1962. She would be withdrawn after only 11 years of service during 1966. (WS6728)

Above: Wednesday 12 June 1963. The Wemyss Private Railway was the operating arm of the Wemyss Coal Company which was absorbed by the National Coal Board during the Nationalisation of the coal industry in January 1947. The railway remained 'independent' and was responsible for transporting the product of a number of collieries which were formerly owned by the Wemyss family. With large collieries at Lochhead, Michael near East Wemyss and the Wellesley at Methil the railway was kept very busy moving coal to the washer at the Wellesley before loading into ships at Methil Dock. The Wellesley closed in July 1967 with the Michael following in September of the same year after an explosion which saw production cease. The Lochhead colliery closed in March 1970 and with this last producer in the area gone the Wemyss Private Railway was closed in June of the same year. This splendid photograph shows Wemyss Private Railway 'Austerity' No. 15 working hard with a train of loaded coal wagons between East Wemyss and Buckhaven. Constructed by Andrew Barclay in 1945 and given the works number 2183 she survived into the preservation scene and is currently operational at the Avon Valley Railway numbered 15 and named *Earl David*. (WS6820)

Thursday 12 September 1963. Ex-LMS Class 5 4-6-0 No. 44998 is approaching Gleneagles station at the head of the 5.20pm two coach working from Crieff. She was a Horwich Works product that entered service during 1947 and would be withdrawn 20 years later in 1967. Allocated new to Crewe North shed, she was re-allocated to Perth in 1948 and would spend the rest of her working life based there. Crieff station was opened by the Crieff Junction Railway in March 1856 but it would not be until May 1905 that the final section westwards was opened to enable trains to reach Balquhidder on the Callander and Oban Railway. This section from Balquhidder to Comrie was closed to passenger traffic during 1951 but the passenger service between Comrie and Gleneagles continued until final closure in July 1964. (WS7107)

Monday 21 October 1963. With the cavernous interior of Princes Street station in Edinburgh looming in the background, a pair of 'Black 5's are awaiting departure times on their respective workings. On the left is No. 45476, bearing a 64C Dalry Road shed code, at the head of the 5.18pm to Glasgow Central via Holytown. A product of Derby Works during 1943 she would be allocated new to Inverness, re-allocated to Perth in 1960 and end her days at Dalry Road from 1961 being withdrawn during 1964. On the right is No. 45214 bearing a 65J Stirling shed code, at the head of the 5.32pm working to Stirling. One of the earlier members of the class entering service during 1935 from Armstrong Whitworth & Co she was initially allocated to English sheds. Moving to Eastfield shed in Glasgow during 1951 the locomotive would end her days based at Corkerhill in Glasgow and be withdrawn in 1966. Constructed between 1890 and 1893, the station at Princes Street in Edinburgh was served with seven platforms all under a huge 850 foot canopy roof. It provided through services to all the main English cities via Carstairs Junction and direct services to Glasgow Central via Shotts and Holytown and also to Lanark. Local branches snaked out to Barnton to the north-west and Balerno in the west of the City with Leith being served by the branch to Leith North. Successive closures took place to Balerno, Barnton and Leith North leaving the station only with connecting services via Carstairs Juncrtion and Glasgow Central. The end came on Saturday 4 September 1965 with the last train departing for Carstairs. The station lay empty for a number of years the platforms becoming useful car parking for the city centre. Demolition followed during 1969 and 1970. (WS7231)

Opposite: Saturday 4 July 1964. The two schoolboys on the platform at Aberdeen station seem to be absorbed in their conversation with a crew member of ex-LNER Class A3 4-6-2 No. 60052 *Prince Palatine*. The fireman has also clearly prepared the locomotive for its start at the head of an Edinburgh bound express. Constructed at Doncaster Works during 1924, numbered 2551 by the LNER and named after the racehorse that won a series of classic races in 1910, 1911, 1912 and 1913, *Prince Palatine* would be one of the last working members of the class based at St Margarets shed in Edinburgh and was withdrawn during 1966. Introduced to the Great Northern railway in 1922, Sir Nigel Gresley's Class A1 locomotives would consist of 52 examples that had been constructed by both Doncaster Works and the North British Locomotive Company in Glasgow, the last entering service in 1925. They were all rebuilt between 1927 and 1948 as Class A3 locomotives with alterations to the boiler and cylinders. Between 1925 and 1935 an additional 27 examples of Class A3 were erected at Doncaster. Designed to handle express passenger traffic throughout the LNER system, they proved themselves to be reliable workhorses. One example has survived, No. 60103 *Flying Scotsman* which at the time of writing is operational and has been working special trains throughout the UK. (WS7550)

Above: Saturday 29 February 1964. On this leap year day, ex-LMS Class 5 4-6-0 No. 44994 is seen at Dalry Middle Junction with the 10.15am Stirling to Edinburgh Princes Street via Larbert working. A product of Horwich Works during 1947 she was initially allocated to Kingmoor shed in Carlisle but would by 1953 be allocated to Dalry Road in Edinburgh and be withdrawn during July 1964. (WS7297)

Opposite top: Monday 25 May 1964. At the head of a long train of empty mineral wagons passing Townhill Junction to the north of Dunfermline is ex-WD Class 8F 2-8-0 No. 90386. Built by the NBL during 1944 and numbered 78592 by the War Department, she would spend time in France during the Second World War and be returned to the U.K. in 1947. The engine was loaned to the LNER in the same year and by 1950 would be allocated to Scottish sheds and end her days based at Dunfermline Upper shed being withdrawn in 1967. (WS7447)

Opposite bottom: Saturday 4 July 1964. On the last day of the passenger service on the Gleneagles to Comrie branch, BR Standard Class 4MT 2-6-4 tank No. 80063 is ready to depart from Crieff station at the head of the 6.45pm working from Comrie to Gleneagles. Constructed at Brighton Works in 1953 she would be withdrawn after only 13 years in 1966. (WS7647)

Above: Saturday 25 July 1964. This fine view overlooking Lundin Links was taken looking west from the footbridge at Largo station and it shows ex-LNER Class B1 4-6-0 No. 61116 at the head of the 12.07pm Thornton Junction to Crail working. Constructed by the NBL during 1947 she would initially be allocated to Eastfield shed in Glasgow but from 1952 until 1962 was allocated to Neasden and Leicester GC sheds. Returning to Eastfield in 1963 she would be withdrawn during 1966. Final closure of the line came in 1969. (WS7599)

Above: Saturday 25 July 1964. At Largo station B1 Class 4-6-0 No 61342 is seen approaching the stop there with a stopper to Crail. Constructed at the former Great Central Railway Gorton Works in 1949 she would be based at Eastfield shed in Glasgow from new and only give 17 years of service being withdrawn during 1966. Of a total of 410 examples of the class which were constructed at Darlington Works, the NBL in Glasgow and the Vulcan Foundry, only ten members of the class were constructed at Gorton Works all entering service during 1948 and 1949. The wooden platform extension opposite to the train may be noted. (WS7601)

Opposite top : Saturday 27 March 1965. Class B1 4-6-0 No. 61330 has worked into Crail earlier in the day and is now waiting in the goods yard with its two coach and one van train to depart as the 2.35pm working to Glasgow Queen Street station. Constructed by the NBL during 1948 she would be allocated new to New England shed but be allocated to Scottish sheds from 1953 ending her days based at Thornton Junction and withdrawn during 1966. (WS7911)

Opposite bottom: Saturday 1 May 1965. Class B1 No. 61330 is seen here again standing at Crail station and waiting to depart with the 2.35pm working to Glasgow Queen Street. (WS7999)

Opposite: Saturday 4 September 1965. In the background the clock on the tower of the North British Hotel shows 1.09pm whilst in the foreground Class B1 4-6-0 No. 61344 is waiting to depart at the head of the 1.18pm local to Crail in Fife. This would be the last occasion that this train would run as the 'East Neuk' line would officially close two days later. No. 61344 was another rare example of the Gorton Works constructed members of the class entering service in 1949, she would spend her working life based at Scottish sheds and be withdrawn in 1966. (WS8314)

Above: Monday 27 September 1965. Standing in the south facing number seven bay platform at Stirling station is ex-LMS Class 5 4-6-0 No. 45359. She is waiting to haul the 3.40pm working to Edinburgh Waverley station. With Princes Street station in Edinburgh being closed completely earlier in September all the ex-CR services into Edinburgh were diverted to Waverley station. Bearing the earlier 63B Stirling shed code plate and with Stirling clearly painted on her buffer beam, the 'Black 5' had been constructed by Armstrong Whitworth & Co during 1937, giving 33 years of service she would be withdrawn in 1967. (WS8336)

Above: Monday 27 September 1965. Pausing at Larbert station at the head of the 2.00pm Dundee West to Glasgow Buchanan Street station express is ex-LNER Class V2 2-6-2 No. 60919. Constructed by Darlington Works during 1941 and allocated new to Heaton shed, she would by way of Gateshead and Tweedmouth sheds end her days based at Dundee Tay Bridge and be withdrawn in 1966. Designed by Sir Nigel Gresley the design originally incorporated a monobloc casting incorporating the steam passages, three cylinders and smoke box saddle thus ensuring a steam tight configuration. In practice cracks started to appear in the casting and the locomotives concerned were rebuilt with three separate cylinders necessitating outside steam pipes. As a mixed traffic design of locomotive they were highly successful with a total of 184 examples being constructed between 1936 and 1944. Darlington Works completed the largest share of the work with 159 examples entering service between 1937 and 1944, Doncaster Works completed 25 examples between 1936 and 1942. (WS8338)

Opposite top: Wednesday 18 May 1966. With a full head of steam ex-NBR Class S (LNER Class J37) 0-6-0 No. 64602 is seen climbing away from Bridge of Dun with the daily goods working from Montrose to Brechin. Constructed by the NBL during 1919 she would be withdrawn from service eleven months after this photograph in April 1967. (WS8586)

Opposite bottom: Saturday 20 August 1966. Standing adjacent at Dundee Tay Bridge shed are ex-NBR Class S (LNER Class J37) 0-6-0 No. 64608 and Class A2 4-6-2 No. 60530 Sayajirao with typical end of steam white embellishments. The J37 was a product of the NBL in 1919 that would be withdrawn from service during the same week as this photograph. The A2 entered service from Doncaster Works in 1948 and would remain in service a few more months being withdrawn during November 1966. (WS8727)

Right: Saturday 15 October 1966. Ex-NBR Class C (LNER Class J36) 0-6-0 No. 65345 has only just been transferred to Thornton Junction shed from Bathgate and the staff at Thornton have given her a 'sprucing up'. She bears no British Railways identity or works plate and the smoke box number has been carefully painted on. Constructed by Cowlairs Works during 1900 and entering service as the penultimate member of the class, she was numbered 793 by the NBR becoming 9793 and later 5345 with the LNER. Rebuilt in the form seen here during 1923 she would give 67 years of service being withdrawn in 1967. (WS8876)

Bottom: October 1966. Ex-WD Class 8F 2-8-0 No. 90117 is laying a smokescreen over Dysart as it departs from the goods yard with a short train of loaded coal wagons. Constructed by the NBL during 1943 as one of the earliest examples of the class to enter service, she would initially be loaned to the LNER before shipping to France in 1945. Returning to the UK in 1947 she would be acquired by British Railways and numbered 90117 by them allocated to Dunfermline Upper shed. She would be withdrawn from service during 1967. Designed by R. A. Riddles for the Ministry of Supply, a staggering total of 935 examples were produced of these 2-8-0s between January 1943 and May 1945 with 545 coming from both the Queens Park and Hyde Park Works of the North British Locomotive Co and 390 from the Vulcan Foundry in Newton-le-Willows. After D-Day they saw service in France, Belgium and Holland and after the end of the war many worked in West Germany. In 1946 the state railway in Holland purchased 184 of these powerful locomotives many staying in service until 1958. Additionally 12 were purchased by the Kowloon and Canton Railway in Hong Kong during 1946 a few remaining in service until 1962. Oddly two examples were purchased by Swedish Railways in 1953 one of which returned to the U.K. when purchased by the Keighley and Worth Valley Railway in 1973. A major overhaul followed starting in 1993 and she was returned to steam during 2007 restored to original condition. (WS8895)